Congressional
Research Service
Informing the legislative debate since 1914 _____

International Food Aid Programs: Background and Issues

Randy Schnepf
Specialist in Agricultural Policy

May 28, 2014

Congressional Research Service

7-5700

www.crs.gov

R41072

Summary

For almost six decades, the United States has played a leading role in global efforts to alleviate hunger and malnutrition and to enhance world food security through international food aid assistance—primarily through either the sale on concessional terms or the donation of U.S. agricultural commodities. Foreign food aid assistance accounts for about 4% of total U.S. foreign aid each year, with economic and military assistance accounting for most outlays. The objectives of foreign food aid include providing emergency and humanitarian assistance in response to natural or manmade disasters, and promoting agricultural development and food security.

U.S. international food aid has traditionally been distributed through five main program authorities: the Food for Peace Act (P.L. 480); the Section 416(b) program; the Food for Progress Act of 1985; the McGovern-Dole International Food for Education and Child Nutrition Program; and the Local and Regional Procurement Pilot Program. These food aid programs are administered either by the Foreign Agricultural Service of the U.S. Department of Agriculture (USDA) or by the U.S. Agency for International Development (USAID). Average annual spending on international food aid programs over the decade FY2002-FY2011 was approximately $2.2 billion, with Food for Peace Title II activities averaging nearly $1.7 billion (or about 80%) of the annual budget. All of these programs—with the exception of Section 416(b), which is permanently authorized by the Agricultural Act of 1949—are traditionally authorized in farm bills. The Section 416(b) program has been inactive since FY2007. The other four major international food aid programs, as well as the Bill Emerson Humanitarian Trust (BEHT)—a reserve of commodities and cash for use in the Food for Peace programs to meet unanticipated food aid needs—were reauthorized through FY2018 by the 2014 farm bill, the Agricultural Act of 2014 (P.L. 113-79).

In addition, the enacted 2014 farm bill amended current food aid law to place greater emphasis on improving the quality of food aid products (i.e., enhancing their nutritional quality) and ensuring that sales of agricultural commodity donations do not disrupt local markets. The 2014 farm bill also repealed the specified, annual dollar amounts for nonemergency food aid—referred to as the "safe box." Instead, it provided that not less than 20%, nor more than 30% of funds be made available to carry out nonemergency food aid programs, subject to the requirement that a minimum of $350 million be provided for nonemergency food aid each fiscal year. P.L. 113-79 also created a new local and regional purchase (LRP) program in place of an expired LRP pilot program, and raised the authorized appropriations for LRP to $80 million annually for FY2014 through FY2018.

While the 2014 farm bill made some modest changes to existing U.S. food aid programs, the Administration had proposed making more sweeping "reforms" to both the structure and intent of U.S. food aid programs as part of its FY2014 budget request. The proposals included shifting funds from Food for Peace to three USAID accounts, eliminating the monetization procedure, providing greater flexibility to procure commodities in local and regional markets overseas, and reducing the volume of commodities subject to cargo preference legislation. USDA and USAID continue to advocate for the Administration's reform agenda, and the President has reintroduced a revised version of his reform proposal in his FY2015 budget request. These reform proposals are being debated as part of the annual appropriations process.

Contents

Figures

Tables

Contacts

Background

For almost six decades, the United States has played a leading role in global efforts to alleviate hunger and malnutrition and to enhance world food security through the provision of international food aid. U.S. food aid programs provide U.S. commodities for emergency food relief and to support development projects.

The U.S. government has provided food aid primarily through five program authorities:

1. Section 416(b) of the Agricultural Act of 1949;

2. Food for Peace Act (historically referred to as P.L. 480);[1]

3. Food for Progress Act of 1985;

4. McGovern-Dole International Food for Education and Child Nutrition (IFECN) Program; and

5. Local and Regional Procurement (LRP) Program.

Section 416(b) is permanently authorized by the Agricultural Act of 1949, whereas the latter four international food aid programs are traditionally reauthorized in periodic farm bills. The 2014 farm bill (P.L. 113-79, the Agricultural Act of 2014), reauthorized these four—along with the Bill Emerson Humanitarian Trust (BEHT), a reserve of commodities and cash for use in the Food for Peace programs to meet unanticipated food aid needs—through FY2018.[2]

While the 2014 farm bill made some modest changes to existing U.S. food aid programs—such as placing greater emphasis on improving the quality of food aid products (i.e., enhancing their nutritional quality) and ensuring that sales of agricultural commodity donations do not disrupt local markets—the Administration had proposed making more sweeping "reforms" to both the structure and intent of U.S. food aid programs.

The President's food aid proposal—first outlined in his FY2014 budget request and discussed in detail below—would have shifted funds previously allocated to Food for Peace Title II emergency and nonemergency food aid, to programs that are authorized in foreign assistance legislation. The Administration proposals were not adopted in the 2014 farm bill; however, USDA and USAID continue to advocate for the Administration's reform agenda, and the President has reintroduced a revised version of his reform proposal in his FY2015 budget request.

This report describes the major U.S. international food aid programs along with the related issues—including the Administration's reform proposals—currently before Congress.

---

[1] The original name of P.L.480 was the Agricultural Trade Development and Assistance Act of 1954 (P.L. 83-480). In 1961, President John F. Kennedy renamed it the "Food for Peace Act." Congress officially changed the name to Food for Peace Act in the 2008 farm bill (P.L. 110-246).

[2] The Bill Emerson Humanitarian Trust was originally authorized by the Agricultural Act of 1980 (P.L. 96-494) as the Food Security Wheat Reserve, but was later reauthorized and renamed by the Africa Seeds of Hope Act of 1989 (P.L. 105-385).

Food Aid Programs

Food aid programs are administered either by the Foreign Agricultural Service (FAS) of the U.S. Department of Agriculture (USDA) or by the U.S. Agency for International Development (USAID). **Table 1** lists the year each international food assistance program was enacted (or first instituted in the case of the EFSP), and the agency responsible for administering each program.

Table 1. U.S. International Food Assistance Programs

Program	Year Began	Implementing Agency
Food for Peace Act, Title I Economic Assistance and Food Security	1954	FAS, USDA
Food for Peace Act, Title II Emergency and Private Assistance	1954	USAID
Food for Peace Act, Title III Food for Development	1990	USAID
Food for Peace Act, Title V Farmer-to-Farmer	1985	USAID
Section 416(b)	1949	FAS, USDA
Food for Progress	1985	FAS, USDA
McGovern-Dole IFECN Program	2003	FAS, USDA
Local & Regional Procurement Program	2008	FAS, USDA
Bill Emerson Humanitarian Trust (BEHT)	1980	FAS, USDA
Emergency Food Security Program (EFSP)	2010	USAID

Source: CRS.

Some of USDA's international activities (Food for Peace Act, McGovern-Dole Food for Education program, and the operations of the FAS itself) are funded through annual Agriculture appropriations acts. Funding for other foreign food aid programs (e.g., Food for Progress, Bill Emerson Humanitarian Trust) is authorized in farm bills and financed through the borrowing authority of USDA's Commodity Credit Corporation (CCC). Congress has occasionally applied limits to spending on these mandatory programs in annual appropriations acts.

Funding for the Emergency Food Security Program (EFSP) is included in USAID's International Disaster Assistance (IDA) account, which is authorized in annual State Department and Foreign Operations appropriations.

Average annual spending on all U.S. international food aid programs during FY2000-FY2009 (not including FAS operations and staff; **Table 2**) was approximately $2.1 billion, with Food for Peace activities comprising the largest component ($1.7 billion or 78%). More recently, for FY2010-FY2012, total U.S. international food aid program spending has declined slightly to about $2 billion, while Food for Peace program annual outlays have grown to about $1.8 billion, or an 88% share.

Table 3 provides program levels for USDA-funded international food aid programs for FY2005-FY2012 (actual outlays), FY2013 and FY2014 (enacted), and FY2014 and FY2015 (requested).

Table 2. U.S. International Food Assistance Outlays Since 1952

(period average: $ million and % of total)

Period	World Total	Food for Peace Act, Title I		Food for Peace Act, Title II		Food for Education		Other Food Assistance	
1952-1959	546	307	56%	240	44%	-	0%	-	0%
1960-1969	1,288	850	66%	458	34%	-	0%	-	0%
1970-1979	1,222	768	63%	454	37%	-	0%	-	0%
1980-1989	1,537	800	52%	712	46%	-	0%	25	2%
1990-1999	1,888	526	28%	876	46%	-	0%	486	26%
2000-2009	2,124	133	6%	1,666	78%	62	3%	264	12%
2010-2012	2,032	35	2%	1,780	88%	103	5%	114	6%

Source: USAID, Detailed Foreign Assistance Data, downloaded on May 9, 2014.

Notes: Period averages compiled by CRS.

Table 3. International Food Aid Program Levels, FY2005-FY2015

($ millions)

Program	Actual Outlays								Enacted		Requested	
	2005	2006	2007	2008	2009	2010	2011	2012	2013	2014	2014	2015
Food for Peace (Title II)	1,973	1,577	1,575	2,643	2,386	2,035	1,660	1,647	1,359	1,466	0[a]	1,400
Section 416(b)	76	20	0	0	0	0	0	0	0	0	0	0
Food for Progress	122	131	147	220	216	148	162	246	243	230	255	240
McGovern-Dole IFEC	90	86	99	99	168	174	206	192	175	185	185	185
Local & Regional Procurement Pilot/Program	—	—	—	0	5	24	23	na	0	0	—[b]	—[c]
TOTAL	2,261	1,814	1,821	2,962	2,775	2,381	2,051	2,085	1,690	1,883	440	1,825

Source: "Actual Outlays" are from: U.S. International Food Assistance Report, Annual, at http://www.usaid.gov/what-we-do/agriculture-and-food-security/food-assistance/resources/united-states-international-food; "Enacted and Requested" amounts are from: USDA, *Annual Budget Summary*, various years.

Note: na = not available.

a.   The FY2014 budget request proposed to replace funding for Food for Peace (P.L. 480) Title II food assistance with an equivalent amount in three USAID assistance accounts: Development Assistance (DA), Community Development and Resilience Fund (CDRF), and Emergency Food Assistance Contingency Fund (EFAC).

b.   The Administration's FY2014 budget request described in the previous table note would have expanded cash availability for emergency response by over $1.4 billion but in the DA, CDRF, and EFAC accounts and not in the local and regional procurement program.

c.   The Administration requested new authority to use up to 25% of total Title II funds (or $350 million of the $1.4 billion requested) for cash-based assistance for emergencies—i.e., local and regional purchases, food vouchers, or cash transfers for procurement of agricultural commodities.

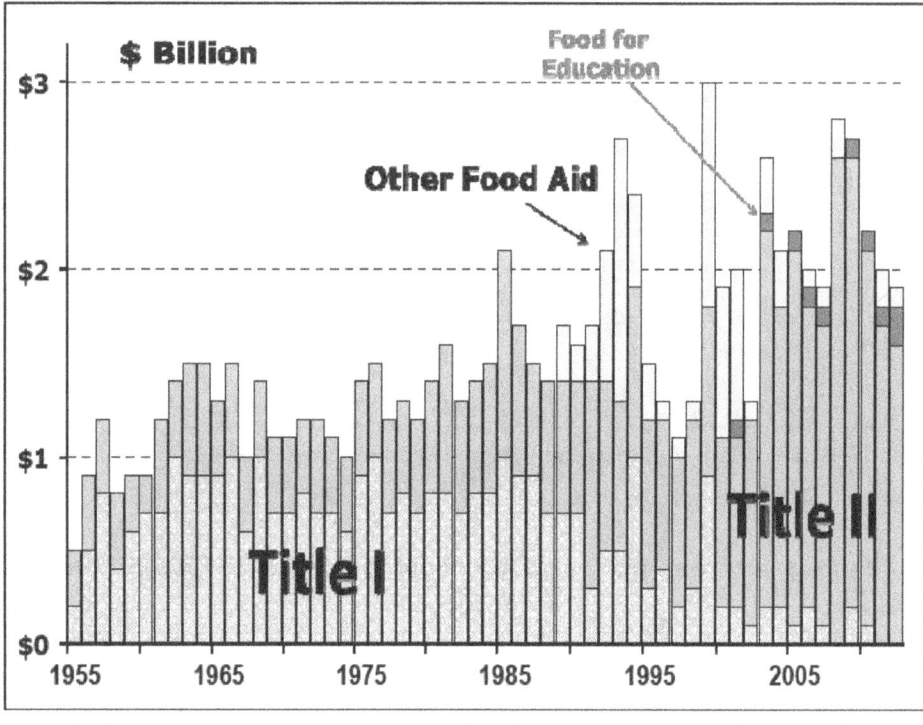

Figure 1. U.S. International Food Assistance Since 1955

Source: U.S. AID, Detailed Foreign Assistance Data, downloaded on May 9, 2014, from http://www.usaid.gov/results-and-data/data-resources.

Food for Peace Act (P.L. 480)[3]

The Food for Peace Act, historically referred to as P.L. 480, is the main legislative vehicle that authorizes foreign food assistance. Since 2000, Food for Peace outlays have accounted for over 85% of total U.S. annual international food aid spending (**Table 2**).[4] Food for Peace Act food aid has five stated objectives: combating world hunger and malnutrition and their causes; promoting sustainable agricultural development; expanding international trade; fostering private sector and market development; and preventing conflicts.

The Food for Peace Act is comprised of four primary programs, which are each listed under a different title and have different objectives. The Food for Peace Act components include:

- **Title I, Economic Assistance and Food Security**, which makes available long-term, low-interest loans to developing countries and private entities for their purchase of U.S. agricultural commodities to support specific projects;

- **Title II, Emergency and Private Assistance**, which provides for the donation of U.S. agricultural commodities to meet emergency and nonemergency food needs;

---

[3] Additional information on Food for Peace Act (P.L. 480) food aid is available at http://www.usaid.gov/what-we-do/agriculture-and-food-security/food-assistance.

[4] Calculations by CRS using USAID data from http://www.usaid.gov/results-and-data/data-resources.

- **Title III, Food for Development**, which makes government-to-government grants available to support long-term growth in the least developed countries; and

- **Title V, Farmer-to-Farmer Program**, which finances short-term volunteer technical assistance to farmers, farm organizations, and agribusinesses in developing and transitional countries.

Title I of the Food for Peace Act is administered by USDA, while Titles II, III, and V are administered by USAID. Funding for Food for Peace Act programs is authorized in annual Agriculture appropriations bills.

During the first 35 years of P.L. 480 (FY1955 through FY1989), Title I funding typically dwarfed that of other programs, but since the mid-1980s it has declined by more than 90% (**Figure 1**). Successive Administrations have not requested funding for any new Title I food aid programs since FY2006. Title III has been inactive since FY2002. In contrast, since the late 1980s Title II has emerged as the largest vehicle for U.S. food aid shipments. This pattern was reinforced by the 1990 farm bill when strengthening global food security was made a formal objective of American food aid.

Food Aid Consultative Group (FACG)

A Food Aid Consultative Group (FACG) advises the USAID Administrator on food aid policy and regulations, especially related to Title II of P.L. 480. The Administrator is expected to meet with the FACG at least twice per year. The 2014 farm bill, in addition to reauthorizing the FACG, added representatives from the processing sector to the group.

FACG membership consists of:

- the USAID Administrator;

- the Under Secretary of Agriculture for Farm and Foreign Agricultural Services;

- the Inspector General for USAID;

- a representative of each private voluntary organization (PVO) and cooperative participating in FPA programs;

- representatives from African, Asian, and Latin-American indigenous nongovernmental organizations (NGOs) as determined appropriate by the Administrator of USAID;

- representatives from U.S. agricultural producer groups;

- representatives from the U.S. agricultural processing sector involved in providing agricultural commodities for programs under this chapter; and

- representatives from the maritime transportation sector involved in transporting agricultural commodities overseas for programs under this chapter.

The 2014 farm bill specified that USAID is to consult with FACG on the implementation of food aid quality provisions (discussed below) and required that USAID provide FACG at least 45 days for review and comment before a proposed regulation handbook or guideline, or revision thereof, becomes final.

Jargon Buster: What are PVOs, NGOs, and Intergovernmental Organizations?

The international development arena is replete with jargon. As an aid to understanding this development jargon, some common terms—used in this report—are defined here. According to the Food for Peace Act:

- **Nongovernmental organization (NGO)** means "an organization that works at the local level to solve development problems in a foreign country in which the organization is located, except that the term does not include an organization that is primarily an agency or instrumentality of the government of the foreign country." [7 U.S.C. 1732(7)]

- **Private voluntary organization (PVO)** means "a not-for-profit, nongovernmental organization (in the case of a U.S. organization, an organization that is exempt from Federal income taxes under section 501(c)(3) of title 26) that receives funds from private sources, voluntary contributions of money, staff time, or in-kind support from the public, and that is engaged in or is planning to engage in voluntary, charitable, or development assistance activities (other than religious activities)." [7 U.S.C. 1732(8)]

According to USAID, PVOs are a subset of the wider NGO community. USAID maintains a registry of PVOs that enables it to identify legitimate partners and ensure that registrants meet the agency's basic partnership requirements. Most PVOs must register with USAID in order to compete for grants and other types of funding. However, certain types of NGOs do not need to register as a PVO, including universities/colleges, local indigenous NGOs, sub-awardees/grantees, private foundations, hospitals, exclusively religious institutions, and organizations applying for awards from the Office of U.S. Foreign Disaster Assistance.[5]

- An **intergovernmental organization** is an organization composed of independent and sovereign states. Examples include any United Nations (U.N.) agency such as the World Food Program (WFP) or the U.N. Children's Fund (UNICEF). The World Bank and the International Monetary Fund (IMF) are also intergovernmental organizations.

Title I, Economic Assistance and Food Security

Title I of the Food for Peace Act provides for sales on credit terms of U.S. agricultural commodities to developing country governments and to private entities for U.S. dollars or for local currencies. Loan agreements under the Title I credit program may provide for repayment terms of up to 30 years with a grace period of up to five years. Donations of Title I commodities can also be made through Food for Progress grant agreements.

No new funding for Title I credit sales and grants has been appropriated since FY2006, although some funding has been provided to administer previously entered into Title I program agreements.

Title II, Emergency and Private Assistance

Title II of the Food for Peace Act provides for donations of U.S. agricultural commodities to meet emergency and nonemergency food needs in foreign countries. Food aid provided under Title II is primarily targeted to vulnerable populations in response to malnutrition, famine, natural disaster, civil strife, and other extraordinary relief requirements. Title II food aid is also used to meet nonemergency economic development needs that address food security.

- **Emergency assistance** is provided through intergovernmental organizations, particularly the United Nations World Food Program (WFP) and PVOs, although commodities may be used in government-to-government programs.

---

[5] For more information see, USAID, PVO Registration, at http://www.usaid.gov/pvo.

- **Nonemergency assistance** may be provided through PVOs, cooperatives, and intergovernmental organizations.

CCC Commodities

Commodities requested under the Food for Peace Act may be furnished from the inventory of USDA's Commodity Credit Corporation (CCC), if available, or purchased in the market.[6] The CCC also finances transportation costs, including both ocean freight and overland transport costs when appropriate. The CCC may also pay for storage and distribution costs for commodities, including pre-positioned commodities, made available to meet urgent or extraordinary relief requirements. Depending on the agreement, commodities provided under the program may be sold in the recipient country and the proceeds used to support development projects, a practice known as "monetization."[7]

Funding

The 2014 farm bill continued the annual authorization level for Title II at $2.5 billion through FY2018—the same as under the 2008 farm bill. As this authorization is discretionary, it is up to annual appropriations bills to set the actual amount of annual Title II funding, which over the five-year life of the 2008 farm bill (FY2008-FY2012) averaged $1.9 billion annually.

Minimum Tonnages

The Food for Peace Act, as amended, mandates that Title II commodity donations provide an annual minimum tonnage level of 2.5 million metric tons (mmt), of which 1.875 mmt (75%) is to be channeled as nonemergency (development) assistance through the eligible organizations. This mandate can be waived by the USAID Administrator, who can make the determination that there is a greater emergency need, and/or that the mandated volume of commodities cannot be used effectively in nonemergency situations.

Emergency versus Nonemergency Uses

In recent years, the volume of Title II emergency food aid has far exceeded the amount of nonemergency or development food aid (see **Figure 2**). This divergence has served to highlight the divide between conflicting interests—emergency versus nonemergency—in the use of U.S. international food aid in general and Title II funds in particular. The past two Administrations

---

[6] The Commodity Credit Corporation is a U.S. government-owned and -operated corporation, created in 1933, with broad powers to support farm income and prices and to assist in the export of U.S. agricultural products. The CCC finances USDA's domestic price and income support programs and its export programs using its permanent authority to borrow up to $30 billion at any one time from the U.S. Treasury.

[7] Authorization for monetization was first included in the Food Security Act of 1985 (P.L. 99-198). Under Section 1111 of that statute, PVOs or cooperatives were permitted to sell (i.e., monetize) for local currencies or dollars an amount of commodities equal to not less than 10% of the total amount of commodities distributed under Title II in any fiscal year. The currency generated by these sales could then be used to finance internal transportation, storage, or distribution of commodities; to implement development projects; or to invest and with the interest earned used to finance distribution costs or projects. This provision has since been amended such that not less than 15% of Title II commodity distribution should be monetized [7 U.S.C. 1723(b)]. This is discussed further later in this report in the section entitled "Monetization".

(Bush and Obama) have both sought greater control over Title II funds in order to direct them to international points of crisis in a more timely manner, thus helping to better meet U.S. foreign policy goals. In contrast, a large number of NGOs and PVOs working in developing countries have come to depend on Title II commodity monetization as a primary source of funds for their operations. These groups represent a very effective lobby for the preservation of nonemergency uses (i.e., monetization). As a result, Congress has included some form of funding guarantee for nonemergency programs in the past two farm bills (the 2008 and 2014 farm bills).

Figure 2. Allocation of Food for Peace Title II Commodities to Emergency and Nonemergency Programs, FY1992-FY2012

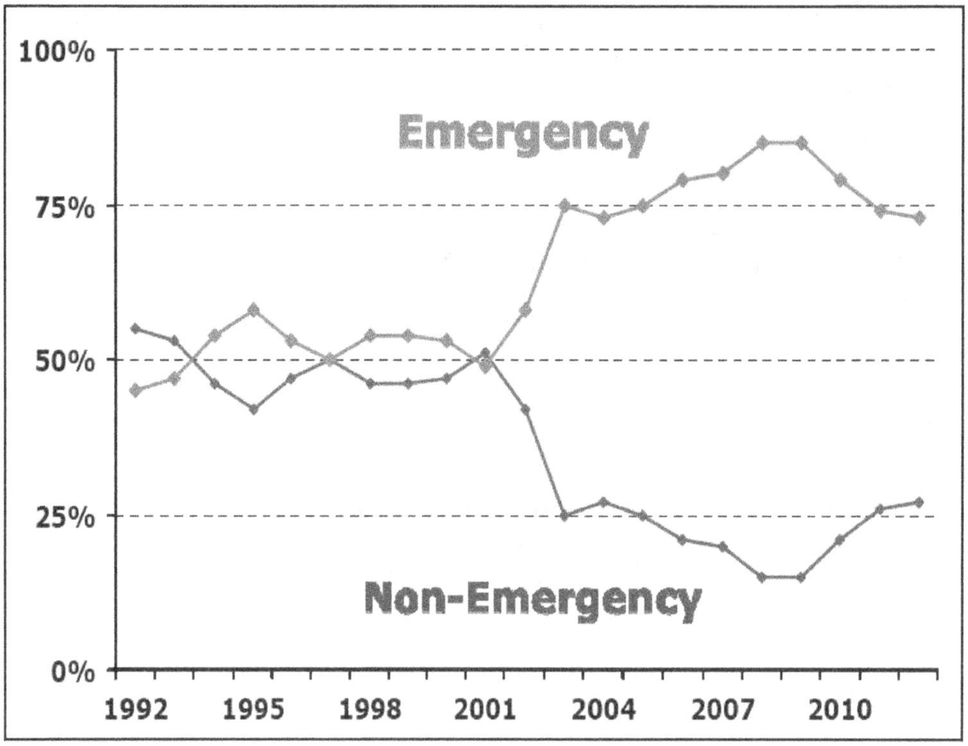

Source: USAID, U.S. International Food Assistance Report, various years.

Note: Data compiled by CRS.

The 2008 farm bill (P.L. 110-246; §3021) established a so-called "safe box" for funding of nonemergency development assistance projects under Title II. The aim of the safe box was to provide assurances to the implementing organizations (PVOs, cooperatives, intergovernmental organizations) of a given level of funds with which to carry out development projects. The safe box funding level ranged from $375 million in FY2009 to $450 million in FY2012 and again in FY2013 under the "fiscal cliff" legislation (P.L. 112-240). The 2014 farm bill (§3012) repealed the specified dollar amounts for nonemergency food aid (i.e., the safe box) and instead provided that not less than 20%, nor more than 30%, of funds be made available to carry out nonemergency food aid programs, subject to the requirement that a minimum of $350 million be provided for nonemergency food aid each fiscal year.

Administration and Monitoring

The 2014 farm bill authorized the use of up to $17 million annually for the monitoring and assessment of nonemergency food aid programs, of which not more than $500,000 may be used in each fiscal year for maintenance of information technology systems. An annual report to Congress is to address how funds are allocated to and used by eligible organizations as well as the rate of return on aid funds—defined as the sum of the proceeds from monetization of food aid commodities relative to the total cost of procuring and shipping the commodities to the recipient country's local market. Special attention is to be given when the rate of return is below 70%.

Food Quality and Prepositioning

The 2014 farm bill also amended current food aid law to place greater emphasis on improving the quality of food aid products—that is, enhancing their nutritional quality[8]—and ensuring that sales of agricultural commodity donations do not disrupt local markets.

In addition, the 2014 farm bill reauthorized pre-positioning of commodities overseas, increased the funding for pre-positioning to $15 million annually from $10 million annually, and allowed USAID to have discretion over whether to establish additional prepositioning sites based on the results of assessments of need, technology, feasibility, and cost. USAID maintains that pre-positioning (at various sites in the United States and around the world) enables it to respond more rapidly to emergency food needs. Critics say, however, that the cost-effectiveness of pre-positioning has not been evaluated.

Title III, Food for Development

Title III, Food for Development, provides for government-to-government grants to support long-term economic development in the least developed countries. Under this program, donated commodities can be sold in the recipient countries (i.e., monetized) and the revenue generated is used to support programs that promote economic development and food security, including development of agricultural markets, school feeding programs, nutrition programs, and infrastructure programs. The costs of procurement, processing, and transportation are also paid for by the U.S. government under Title III.

No funding request has been made for Title III activities since FY2002.

Title V, Farmer-to-Farmer Program (FtF)

The Farmer-to-Farmer program, first authorized in the 1985 farm bill, has been reauthorized in subsequent farm bills, including the 2014 farm bill.[9] The FtF program does not provide commodity food aid, but instead provides technical assistance to farmers, farm organizations, and agribusinesses in developing and transitional countries. The program mobilizes the expertise of

---

[8] Discussed in more detail later in this report in the section entitled "Food Aid Quality".

[9] The 2008 farm bill designated this program as the "John Ogonowski and Doug Bereuter Farmer-to-Farmer Program" in honor of one of the pilots killed September 11, 2001, who was also a participant in the program, and of former Representative Bereuter, a supporter of the program.

volunteers from U.S. farms, land grant universities, cooperatives, private agribusinesses, and nonprofit organizations to carry out short-term projects overseas.

The 2014 farm bill provided minimum funding for the program of the greater of $15 million or 0.6% of the funds made available to Food for Peace Act programs for each year from FY2014 through FY2018. In addition, the 2014 farm bill added a requirement for a Government Accountability Office (GAO) report to review the program and provide recommendations to improve the monitoring and evaluation of the program.

Other Food Aid Programs

Section 416(b)[10]

The Section 416(b) program, which is permanently authorized by the Agricultural Act of 1949, provides for the overseas donation of surplus agricultural commodities owned by the CCC. The program is administered by USDA and has been a highly variable component of food aid because it is entirely dependent on the availability of surplus commodities in CCC inventories.

By the late 1940s, the U.S. government had accumulated huge stocks of wheat and corn as part of its price support programs. These large stocks depressed market prices and contributed to a vicious cycle of government support payments and stock accumulation. The Section 416(b) program was designed, in part, to help draw down government stocks by donating and shipping surplus government-owned commodities to foreign countries that lacked sufficient buying power to participate in commercial markets. Changes to federal price support programs made in the mid-1980s (i.e., special marketing loan program benefits) were designed to preclude further government stock accumulation of program crops. As a result, government grain stocks were eventually depleted by 2006.

Under its statutory authority, Section 416(b) donations may not reduce the amounts of commodities that traditionally are donated to domestic feeding programs or agencies, and may not disrupt normal commercial sales. The commodities are made available for donation through agreements with foreign governments, PVOs, cooperatives, and intergovernmental organizations. Depending on the agreement, the commodities donated under Section 416(b) may be sold in the recipient country and the proceeds used to support agricultural, economic, or infrastructure development programs.

The Section 416(b) program has been inactive since FY2007 because of the unavailability of CCC-owned stocks.

Food for Progress (FFP)[11]

The Food for Progress (FFP) program was authorized in the Food for Progress Act of 1985 and is administered by USDA's Foreign Agricultural Service. The program authorizes the CCC to carry

---

[10] For more information visit, http://apps.fas.usda.gov/excredits/FoodAid/416b/section416b.asp.

[11] [7 U.S.C. 1736o] Additional information on the Food for Progress program is available at http://www.fas.usda.gov/programs/food-progress.

out the sale and export of U.S. agricultural commodities on credit terms or on a grant basis, using either CCC financing or Title I funds. The program is intended to assist developing countries and emerging democracies to strengthen free enterprise development in the agricultural sector. FFP focuses especially on private sector development of agricultural infrastructure, such as improved agricultural production practices, marketing systems, farmer training, agro-processing, and agribusiness development.

Eligible implementing organizations request commodities and USDA purchases those commodities from the U.S. market. Then USDA donates the commodities to the implementing organizations and pays for the freight to move the commodity to the recipient country. Organizations eligible to carry out FFP programs include governments, PVOs, cooperatives, and intergovernmental organizations, such as the World Food Program (WFP).

Not less than 400,000 metric tons of commodities shall be provided each fiscal year in the FFP program. However, FFP is limited by statute to pay no more than $40 million annually for freight costs. In FY2013, FFP programs valued at nearly $172 million were targeted to nearly 4 million beneficiaries through various implementing partners in 10 developing countries.[12]

McGovern-Dole International Food for Education and Child Nutrition (IFECN) Program[13]

The McGovern-Dole IFECN program was first authorized in the 2002 farm bill (P.L. 107-171), the Farm Security and Rural Investment Act of 2002, and is administered by USDA's Foreign Agricultural Service.[14] The program uses commodities and financial and technical assistance to carry out school feeding programs and maternal, infant, and child nutrition programs in foreign countries. The 2014 farm bill reauthorized the program through FY2018 with "such sums as are necessary" to administer the program.

The commodities used in the program are made available for donation through agreements with PVOs, cooperatives, intergovernmental organizations, and foreign governments. Commodities may be donated for direct feeding or, in limited situations, for local sale to generate proceeds to support school feeding and nutrition projects. Priority countries under the McGovern-Dole IFECN program must demonstrate sufficient need for improving domestic nutrition, literacy, and food security.

In FY2012, the McGovern-Dole IFECN program, valued at $191.7 million, provided 66,224 metric tons of commodities (e.g., soybean oil, rice, potatoes, lentils, wheat, dark red kidney beans, soybean meal, corn soy blend, and other) to nearly 3.8 million beneficiaries in 17 developing countries in Asia, Africa, and Latin America.[15]

---

[12] Available at http://www.fas.usda.gov/programs/food-progress/food-progress-funding-allocations-fy-2013; for a list of active FFP projects see http://www.fas.usda.gov/programs/food-progress/active-food-progress-projects.

[13] 7 U.S.C. 1736o-1. Additional information on the McGovern-Dole IFECN program is available at http://www.fas.usda.gov/programs/mcgovern-dole-food-education-program.

[14] This program is named in honor of former ambassador and former Senator George McGovern and former Senator Robert Dole for their efforts to encourage a global commitment to school feeding and child nutrition.

[15] "Appendix H: McGovern-Dole International Food for Education and Child Nutrition Program—Fiscal Year 2012 Donations by Country and Commodity," at http://www.fas.usda.gov/sites/default/files/fy_2012_ifar_final.pdf.

Local and Regional Procurement (LRP) Program[16]

Initially authorized as a pilot project by the 2008 farm bill with $60 million in annual funding, the Local and Regional Procurement (LRP) project was authorized as a permanent program under the 2014 farm bill with annual CCC funding of $80 million for each of FY2014 through FY2018. The primary purpose of the LRP program is to expedite the provision of food aid to vulnerable populations affected by food crises and disasters. A secondary purpose is to provide development assistance that will enhance the food consumption security of such populations.

The LRP program is administered by USDA. Under the program, grants are provided to PVOs, cooperatives, and the WFP to undertake the procurement activities. Preference in carrying out this program may be given to eligible organizations that have, or are working toward, projects under the McGovern-Dole IFECN program. USDA is required to submit an annual report to Congress on the LRP program's implementation time frame, costs, and impact on local and regional producers, markets, and consumers.

Under the earlier LRP Pilot Project, FAS carried out a mandated study on the prior experience of other donor countries, PVOs, and the WFP with local and regional procurement, and submitted a report to Congress in January 2009.[17] The agency released interim guidelines in September 2009.[18] Pilot field-based projects were then completed. USDA's evaluation report, conducted by Management Systems International and Coffey International Development, was published in December 2012.[19] The evaluation found that total time for LRP purchases averaged 56 days, while total time for comparable in-kind shipments to the same countries in the same time frame took an average of 130 days, that is, 74 days longer for in-kind commodities to arrive. (Evaluators did not have data on pre-positioned in-kind stocks to compare delivery times of LRP with delivery times of prepositioned in-kind commodities.) The evaluation found that for five commodity categories (unprocessed cereals, milled cereals, fortified blended foods, pulses, and vegetable oils), the in-kind commodity costs were lower than LRP commodity costs when counting commodity cost alone. However, total costs (which included ocean, inland, and internal transport, storage, and handling as well as commodity costs) were lower for LRP for every commodity category except for vegetable oils.[20]

The Bill Emerson Humanitarian Trust (BEHT)[21]

The Bill Emerson Humanitarian Trust (BEHT) is a reserve of U.S. commodities and cash authorized under the Africa: Seeds of Hope Act of 1998 (P.L. 105-385). The trust is not a food

---

[16] 7 U.S.C. 1726c. Additional information about the USDA's Local and Regional Procurement Project is available at http://www.fas.usda.gov/excredits/FoodAid/LRP/LRP.asp.

[17] A copy of the study report, which USDA released to Congress in January 2009, is available at http://www.fas.usda.gov/excredits/FoodAid/LRP/USDALRPStudy.pdf.

[18] Interim guidelines are available at http://www.fas.usda.gov/excredits/FoodAid/LRP/Interim_PPP_Guidelines.pdf.

[19] *USDA Local and Regional Food Aid Procurement Pilot Project*, Independent Evaluation Report, December 2012, viewed at http://www.fas.usda.gov/info/LRP%20Annexes%2012-12-12%20TO%20PRINT.pdf.

[20] For additional background and discussion about issues related to local and regional procurement, see CRS Report R40759, *Local and Regional Procurement for U.S. International Emergency Food Aid*.

[21] 7 U.S.C. 1736f-1. Bill Emerson, a Member of Congress from Missouri, was the ranking Member of the House Select Committee on Hunger. Additional information on the Emerson Trust is available at http://www.fas.usda.gov/programs/bill-emerson-humanitarian-trust.

aid program per se, but rather a food reserve that can be used to meet unanticipated humanitarian food aid needs in developing countries. The trust replaced the Food Security Commodity Reserve established in the 1996 farm bill and its predecessor, the Food Security Wheat Reserve, originally authorized by the Agricultural Trade Act of 1980. The 2014 farm bill reauthorized the BEHT through FY2018. The program is administered under the authority of the Secretary of Agriculture.

Since 1980, the only commodity held in reserve has been wheat. The 2008 farm bill removed the previous 4 million ton cap on commodities that can be held in the trust, and provides the Secretary with the ability to exchange commodities in the trust for cash, provided the sale does not disrupt markets. It also allows the Secretary to invest the funds from the trust in low-risk, short-term securities or instruments so as to maximize its value. During 2008, USDA sold the remaining wheat in the trust (about 915,000 MT) so that currently the BEHT holds only cash (about $311 million in FY2013). The cash can be used to finance activities or purchase commodities to meet emergency food needs when FPA Title II funds are not available.

USDA's Commodity Credit Corporation (CCC) may be reimbursed for the value of U.S. commodities released from the Emerson Trust from either P.L. 480 appropriations or direct appropriations for reimbursement. The CCC may then use that reimbursement to replenish commodities released. Reimbursement to the CCC for ocean freight and related non-commodity costs occurs through the regular USDA appropriations process.

Emergency Food Security Program (EFSP)

The Emergency Food Security Program (EFSP) provides grants for local and regional procurement of food commodities, or the use of cash or vouchers for the purchase of food in response to an emergency. EFSP was started in FY2010 to complement USAID's in-kind food aid.[22] USAID initiated EFSP to respond to the highest priority emergency food security needs as a complement to the Food for Peace Title II emergency food aid program.[23]

USAID uses funds from its International Disaster Assistance (IDA) account, authorized under the Foreign Assistance Act of 1961, to finance EFSP activities. Up to $300 million in IDA funds were made available for the EFSP in each of FY2010 and FY2011. In FY2012 up to $380 million of IDA funds were made available for the EFSP. Implementing partners include U.S. and foreign NGOs, cooperatives, and intergovernmental organizations. No EFSP funds have been provided via developing country governments.

EFSP uses IDA funds to finance three kinds of emergency food security assistance:

- **Local and Regional Procurement (LRP)**. Funds are used to purchase food commodities within the disaster-affected country or from a nearby country for distribution in the disaster-affected country.

---

[22] USAID, "Fiscal Year 2012 Emergency Food Security Program Fact Sheet," available at http://www.usaid.gov/what-we-do/agriculture-and-food-security/food-assistance/programs/emergency-programs.

[23] This discussion of USAID's Emergency Food Security Program is based on USAID/Bureau for Democracy, Conflict, and Humanitarian Assistance/Office of Food for Peace Annual Program Statement for International Emergency Food Assistance, Opp. No. APS-FFP-13-000001, issued May 6, 2013; at http://www.usaid.gov/sites/default/files/documents/1866/FY13%20USAID%20APS-FFP-13-000001.pdf.

- **Cash Transfers**. Cash is provided to disaster-affected people for use in purchasing essential food items to meet their food security needs. Cash transfers can take the form of a physical payment or an electronic transfer through mobile providers or financial institutions.

- **Food Vouchers**. Local food vendors supply specific essential food items to beneficiaries through paper or electronic food vouchers.

According to USAID, it uses EFSP funds when U.S.-purchased Food for Peace Title II food aid cannot arrive fast enough to respond to an emergency or when local procurement, cash transfers, or food voucher programs may be more appropriate than U.S. in-kind food aid due to local market conditions (**Table 4** and **Table 5**).

Table 4. Emergency Food Security Program (EFSP), FY2010-FY2012

	FY2010	FY2011	FY2012
Program Value ($ million)	$244	$232	$374
Metric Tons of Food Delivered	278,870	191,616	177,346
Programs Funded	17	30	45
Countries Receiving Assistance	8	21	19
Beneficiaries Assisted (millions)	15.5	19.7	10.7

Source: See source notes below.

Table 5. F2011-FY2012 EFSP Breakdown

(% of fiscal year program value from **Table 4**)

	FY2011	FY2012
Local/Regional Purchase	79%	44%
Food Vouchers	9%	14%
Cash Transfers	12%	42%
Total	100%	100%

Source: USAID Emergency Food Security Program Fact Sheets for FY2011 and for FY2012.

Note: For FY2012, Cost per metric ton of local and regional purchase = $929/mt = ($164.8 M)/(17,7346 mt).

Issues for Congress

Food aid issues currently being debated include assuring the nutritional quality and safety of food aid products; the effects of monetization, or selling U.S. agricultural commodities to finance development projects of nongovernmental organizations; local and regional procurement of food aid commodities versus procurement in the United States; and the effects of cargo preference legislation on food aid program costs. Some of the issues were addressed in the 2014 farm bill. The Administration's food aid reform proposals represent another approach to addressing these issues.

Food Aid Quality

Concerns about the nutritional quality and safety of food aid have been raised in recent analyses of U.S. food aid programs.[24] These studies point to reduced food aid budgets, high and volatile food prices, and frequent and protracted humanitarian emergencies as factors underlying a need for greater attention to the nutritional content of U.S. food aid.[25]

Historically, most U.S. food aid has been delivered in the form of general rations composed of unfortified grains and legumes (wheat, corn, sorghum, rice, soybeans, peas, lentils, and vegetable oils). Estimates are that about 25% of the volume of U.S. food aid is in the form of fortified blended foods (FBFs).[26] Advances in food and nutritional sciences in recent years, including the development of improved product formulations and new products, have enhanced the capacity of food aid providers to deliver more nutritious foods to target groups such as children or lactating mothers or HIV-positive individuals. Not only have new FBF formulations been created, but also new products such as ready to use therapeutic foods (RUTFs), including lipid-based products, have been developed.[27]

GAO's 2011 report noted two significant challenges in delivering more nutritional products to food aid recipients. One is that specialized food products are generally more expensive than food rations used in general distribution feeding program. According to GAO, a typical ration consisting of rice, cornmeal, wheat, or sorghum could range in cost from $0.02 per day for a 6-month old child to $0.09 per day for a 2-year-old child. A daily ration of FBFs which includes additional fortification could cost between $0.06 and $0.12 per day, depending on the size of the ration. Within a fixed budget, GAO noted, providing more expensive specialized products would reduce the number of people fed.

A second challenge, according to GAO, is that U.S. food aid agencies poorly target the specialized food aid products provided. In this connection, GAO notes that USAID provides implementing partners with limited guidance on how to target more nutritious foods to ensure they reach intended recipients.

GAO recommends that USAID and USDA issue guidance to implementing partners on addressing nutritional deficiencies, especially during protracted emergencies, and evaluate the

---

[24] U.S. Government Accountability Office (GAO*), International Food Assistance: Better Nutrition and Quality Control Can Further Improve U.S. Food Aid*, GAO-11-491, May 2011, viewed at http://gao.gov/assets/320/318210.pdf; and Patrick Webb et al., *Improving the Nutritional Quality of U.S. Food Aid: Recommendations for Changes to Products and Programs:* report to USAID, prepared by Tufts University, Friedman School of Nutrition and Policy, 2011, viewed at http://nutrition.tufts.edu/documents/ImprovingtheNutritionalQuality.pdf.

[25] In addition to nutritional aspects of food aid, food aid quality also includes food safety, sensory aspects such as taste, smell and texture, and convenience, such as ease of cooking.

[26] FBFs are foods that are complementary to typical rations of grains and legumes. They contain both calories and proteins and are fortified with essential micronutrients. FBFs are usually pre-cooked and are designed for use in programs where older infants and young children are being fed. For detailed information on FBFs, see World Food Programme, "Food Quality Control, Food Specifications: Blended Food Products," viewed at http://foodquality.wfp.org/FoodSpecifications/BlendedFoodsFortified/tabid/105/Default.aspx.

[27] Therapeutic foods are foods designed for specific, usually nutritional, therapeutic purposes as a form of dietary supplement. Therapeutic foods are used for emergency feeding of malnourished children or to supplement the diets of persons with special nutritional requirements, such as the elderly or HIV patients. Lipid-based products, like peanut butter-based Plumpy'Nut or Plumpy'Doz, are RUTFs used widely in child feeding programs.

performance and cost effectiveness of specialized food products. The Tufts report to USAID suggests, among other recommendations, that the agency should adopt new specifications for FBFs and explore the use of new products such as new lipid-based products; provide new program guidance to implementing partners; and convene an interagency food aid committee to provide technical guidance about specialized products and to interface with industry and implementing partners.

In response to these studies, the 2014 farm bill requires that USAID use Title II funds to assess types and quality of agricultural commodities donated as food aid; adjust products and formulation, as necessary to meet nutrient needs of target populations; test prototypes; adopt new specifications or improve existing specifications for micronutrient food aid products, based on latest development in food and nutrition science; develop new program guidance for eligible organizations to facilitate improved matching of products to purposes; develop improved guidance on how to address nutritional efficiencies among long-term recipients of food aid; and evaluate the performance and cost-effectiveness of new/modified food products and program approaches to meet nutritional needs of vulnerable groups.

In the managers' statements to the 2014 farm bill,[28] the managers stated that they expect USAID to set verifiable goals and to maximize strong public-private partnerships with food manufacturers and other stakeholders to more quickly address the deficiencies highlighted in the GAO 2011 report by using currently available studies on food aid quality and nutrition. Also, the managers encouraged USAID to establish multi-year approaches to the procurement of high-value products. Longer-term procurement, to the extent practicable, was expected to encourage investment of specialized equipment needed to deliver critical products in a timely and cost-effective manner. In recognition of the importance associated with close collaboration between USDA and USAID on approving new products, the managers stated that they expect both agencies to adopt clear guidelines to facilitate the swift adoption of new products in order to quickly capture the benefits of the research and testing undertaken in this area.

Monetization

Monetization is the act of selling P.L. 480 donated food aid commodities—purchased in the United States and shipped primarily on U.S.-flag vessels—in the local or regional markets of a recipient country. The sales are generally undertaken by participating international PVOs—many of which are U.S.-based NGOs—which then use the funds generated by these sales to finance their own operations, which may include internal transportation, storage, or distribution of commodities; implementation of development projects; or reinvestment of the funds and subsequent use of the interest earned to finance distribution costs or projects.

U.S. food aid legislation allows PVOs to monetize P.L. 480 commodities in an amount not less than 15% of the aggregate amounts of all commodities distributed under Title II nonemergency programs for each fiscal year.[29] Monetization of in-kind donations was first introduced by the 1985 farm bill (Food Security Act of 1985, P.L. 99-198) which established a minimum level of 10%, which was increased to 15% by the 1996 farm bill (P.L. 104-127). Over time, many of the

---

[28] Available at http://docs.house.gov/billsthisweek/20140127/CRPT-113hrpt-HR2642-SOM.pdf.

[29] 7 U.S.C. 1723(b).

participating PVOs have become dependent on monetized funds as one of their major sources of development finance.

Critics of the practice argue that:

- it is too slow a process to be used effectively in responding to emergencies—by relying on U.S.-based commodities delivered on U.S.-flag vessels due to cargo preference law (discussed below), the process of monetization adds several months to the final delivery of in-country assistance and should be limited to long-term development projects;

- it is far more costly than direct cash transfers for local and regional purchase— studies suggest that relying on U.S.-based commodities delivered on U.S.-flag vessels adds 25% to 50% to the per-unit delivery cost of final assistance, thus shortchanging U.S. taxpayers; and

- it stymies the development of local agricultural markets by depressing commodity prices when in-kind donations are sold into those local markets—this sends the wrong signal to local agricultural producers, thus diminishing the recipient country's ability to develop its own sustainable food systems and hurting economic development in the longer term.

Program assessments by GAO have documented some of the inefficiencies associated with monetization. For example, a 2011 GAO study supports the claim that monetized food aid has the potential to displace commercial trade in recipient countries. Despite legislation that imposes assessments of a country's usual marketing requirements (UMRs) and analyses (Bellmon analyses) of the impact of food aid on local markets,[30] GAO and others report that there nevertheless is significant evidence of negative effects on local markets.[31] Using data from 2008-2011, GAO found that in more than a quarter of countries reviewed, monetized food aid comprised more than 25% of the commercial import volume of specific commodities in recipient countries. In half of these cases, the volume of monetized food exceeded reported commercial imports of the particular commodity by over 100%. GAO also has reported that the average "cost recovery" (the difference between the amount of appropriated funds used to purchase the commodities and the proceeds available for development projects from monetization) ranges from 58% to 76% in USDA- and USAID-sponsored projects, respectively.

In light of these research findings and criticisms, both the Bush and Obama Administrations have sought greater flexibility in their use of Food for Peace Title II funds, but the recommended changes proved controversial as the PVOs that have come to depend on monetized funds pushed back.

---

[30] UMR analyses are undertaken to ensure that U.S. food aid commodities will not affect world commodity prices and/or disrupt commercial trade; Bellmon analyses are used to determine if U.S. food aid shipments will interfere with recipient country production or marketing and if there is adequate storage available in the recipient country.

[31] GAO, *International Food Assistance: Funding Development Projects through the Purchase, Shipment and Sale of U.S. Commodities is Inefficient and Can Cause Adverse Market Impacts*, GAO-11-636, June 2011; and C. B. Barrett and Daniel G. Maxwell, *Food Aid after Fifty Years: Recasting Its Role*, London and New York: Routledge, 2005, pp. 133-138.

However, these Administration efforts are not without their own critics, including the Alliance for Global Food Security,[32] an organization representing 13 PVOs that have been involved in implementing Food for Peace nonemergency programs and one group that advocates for U.S. food aid policies. The U.S. maritime sector has also been critical of Administration proposals for food aid reform. A recent report, commissioned by the Alliance for Global Food Security, evaluated food aid monetization cases in five developing countries.[33] The evaluation's conclusion was that "monetization can lead to benefits beyond those that would be created via direct program funding by addressing credit, hard currency, small volume, and other constraints to buying on the international market, thereby creating business opportunities and increasing the availability of the commodity in the recipient country."[34] Another study found that very small, targeted monetization, as opposed to open market sales to generate cash, can be used as a means to develop capacity of smaller traders to participate in markets, increasing competition and /or combatting price volatility.[35] A survey of U.S. and other food aid programs over a 50-year period suggests, however, that examples of targeted monetization, as opposed to open market sales to generate cash, are few.[36]

Unlike the Alliance for Global Food Security, several of the larger international development PVOs, including CARE International and the Catholic Relief Services, have become skeptical of monetization as a development strategy. In the summer of 2007, CARE International, which had been a major supporter of monetization in the past, announced that it would transition away from the practice of monetization and refuse food commodity donations worth tens of millions of dollars. [37] According to CARE, monetization is management-intensive, costly, fraught with legal and financial risks, and economically inefficient. "Purchasing food in the U.S., shipping it overseas, and then selling it to generate funds for food security programs is far less cost-effective than the logical alternative—simply providing cash to fund food security programs." [38] Finally, CARE echoed criticisms of food aid heard in WTO Doha Round negotiations by noting that when monetization involves open-market sale of commodities to generate cash, which is almost always the case, it inevitability causes commercial displacement. As such, it can be harmful to traders and local farmers and undermine the development of local markets, and can be detrimental to longer-term food security objectives.

Catholic Relief Services—another large PVO—has taken a similar position with respect to monetization, but has not yet decided to transition away from the practice completely. In a recent policy declaration, the organization recognized that selling commodities (monetization) is an inefficient method of obtaining funding.[39] As a consequence, it sells commodities only when it

---

[32] The Alliance for Global Food Security consists of 14 PVOs, cooperatives, and a hunger advocacy group who are involved in U.S. food assistance programs. The organizations are listed at http://foodaid.org/about/.

[33] Informa Economics, *The Value of Food Aid Monetization: Benefits, Risks and Best Practices*, prepared for the Alliance for Global Food Security, November 2012, viewed at http://foodaid.org/news/wp-content/uploads/2012/11/Informa-Economics-Study-Value-of-Food-Aid-Monetization-November-2012.pdf.

[34] *Ibid.*, p. 2.

[35] See A. Abdulai, C. B. Barrett, and P. Hazell, "Food Aid for Market Development in Sub-Saharan Africa," DSGD Working Paper No. 5, International Food Policy Research Institute, viewed at http://wwww.ifpri.org/sites/default/files/publications/dsgdp05.pdf.

[36] GAO and Barrett and Maxwell, op. cit.

[37] See *White Paper on Food Aid Policy*, CARE USA, June 6, 2006, at http://www.care.org/newsroom/articles/2005/12/food_aid_whitepaper.pdf.

[38] Ibid.

[39] See Catholic Relief Services, *The International U.S. Food Aid Program*, viewed at http://crs.org/public-policy/pl-(continued...)

has determined that there are no alternative methods of funding and that the sale will have no negative impacts on local markets and local production. Catholic Relief Services says that its policy is to seek to replace monetization with cash funding to cover program costs.

Local or Regional Procurement (LRP)

The U.S. food aid program is often criticized as an inefficient way to meet the objectives of relieving emergency food needs or fostering economic and agricultural development in receiving countries. Critics point to delayed arrivals of up to four months or more when U.S. commodities are shipped in response to emergency situations. Moreover, ocean transportation costs can be high, particularly on U.S.-flag vessels. GAO concluded that between 2001 and 2008, WFP food aid obtained by local procurement (i.e., closer to the targeted source of need) reduced costs and improved timeliness of delivery, relative to similar food aid that USAID purchased and shipped from the United States to the same countries.[40] In FY2006, USAID estimated that almost half of its food aid allocations went to paying the cost of transportation (ocean transport and internal shipping costs).[41] Ocean freight rates vary from year to year, but paying such costs is one reason that both USDA and USAID in various budget requests proposed the allocation of some portion of Title II emergency funds be made available to purchase commodities in areas near the emergency so as to lower their cost and expedite delivery.

According to USAID, research has shown that cash-based food security assistance can get food to people in critical need 11 to 14 weeks faster than commodity shipments from the United States, and at savings of 25% to 50% .

Congressional and other critics of local purchase maintain that allowing non-U.S. commodities to be purchased with U.S. funds would result in undermining the coalition of commodity groups, PVOs, and shippers that support the program, and in reductions in U.S. food aid.[42] Critics of local or regional procurement also argue that buying locally or regionally could result in price spikes that would make it difficult for poor people to buy the supplies they need on local markets. Some also argue that the reliability and quality of food supplies could not be guaranteed with local or regional procurement.

Since 2002, appropriations for Title II of the Food for Peace Act have averaged $2 billion annually, none of which could be used to purchase foreign-grown food. However, from 2001 to 2008, through programs funded under a different authority, the Foreign Assistance Act, the U.S. government provided approximately $220 million in total cash contributions to WFP that were used to purchase foreign-grown commodities. In addition, in supplemental appropriations for FY2008 and FY2009, Congress provided USAID with $125 million for LRP.

(...continued)

480-title-ii.cfm.

[40] GAO concluded that local procurement was less costly in sub-Saharan Africa and Asia by 34% and 29%, respectively, and reduced aid delivery time by over 100 days for many countries in sub-Saharan Africa. See U.S. Government Accountability Office, *Local and Regional Procurement Can Enhance the Efficiency of U.S. Food Aid, But Many Challenges May Constrain Its Implementation*, GAO-09-570, May 2009, http://www.gao.gov/new.items/d09570.pdf.

[41] USAID FY2006 Congressional Budget Justification.

[42] See H.Rept. 109-255 on H.R. 2744, the FY2006 Agriculture Appropriations Act.

In 2008, the Bush Administration proposed that Congress provide legislative authorization in the farm bill to use up to 25% of annual Title II funds to procure food from selected developing countries near the site of a crisis. The Administration justified this proposal on the grounds that the U.S. response to food emergencies would be more efficient and cost-effective if commodities could be procured locally. The Administration's budget request cited instances in which the U.S. food aid response to emergencies would have been enhanced with this kind of authority, particularly for Iraq in 2003, the Asian tsunami in 2004, Southern and West Africa in 2005, and East Africa in 2006. The Administration was careful to note that "U.S. grown food will continue to play the primary role and will be the first choice in meeting global needs." Local and regional purchases would be made only where the speed of the arrival of food aid is essential, according to USDA. Similarly, in its 2014 food aid reform proposal (discussed below), the Obama Administration proposed even greater legislative flexibility in the use of Title II funds for LRP.

The 2008 farm bill (P.L. 110-246) included a scaled-down version of the Bush Administration's proposal for legislative authority to use up to $300 million of appropriated Title II (P.L. 480) funds for local or regional purchase of emergency food aid. The farm bill provided that a pilot project be conducted by the Secretary of Agriculture with a total of $60 million in mandatory CCC funding (not from P.L. 480 appropriations) during FY2009-FY2012—broken out as $5 million in FY2009; $25 million in FY2010, $25 million in FY2011, and $5 million in FY2012.

Subsequent evaluations of the LRP pilot projects confirmed that LRP could both lower the costs and improve the timeliness of providing food aid in most emergency situations.[43] However, while there are clear advantages of LRP over in-kind food aid in many situations, evaluations of U.S. and other LRP projects recommended that such procurement should be accompanied by careful assessment and monitoring to ensure that concerns about food quality, local market disruption, and assuredness of supply are addressed.

In response to the success of the LRP pilot projects, the 2014 farm bill (P.L. 113-79) converted the expired LRP pilot project into a permanent local and regional purchase (LRP) program and raised the authorized appropriations to $80 million annually for FY2014 through FY2018. The permanent LRP program is intended to complement existing food aid programs, especially the McGovern-Dole program. As a result, preference in carrying out the new LRP program could be given to eligible organizations that have, or are working toward, projects under the McGovern-Dole program. In addition, the 2014 farm bill required that USAID produce an annual report for Congress on the LRP program's implementation time frame, costs, and impact on local and regional producers, markets, and consumers.

Cargo Preference

The cargo preference issue also is related to the question of the cost-effectiveness of providing U.S. commodities as food aid. Ocean transport of government-generated shipments is governed

---

[43] J. L. Fisher, "USDA Local and Regional Procurement Pilot Project: Updates and Next Steps," presentation to the LRP Learning Alliance Lessons Learned Workshop, September 19-22, 2011, Nairobi, Kenya; Erin C. Lentz, Simone Passarelli, Christopher B. Barrett, "The Timeliness and Cost-Effectiveness of the Local and Regional Procurement of Food Aid," Cornell University Working Paper, February 2012; Erin C. Lentz, Christopher B. Barrett and Miguel I. Gómez, "The Impacts of Local and Regional Procurement of US Food Aid: Learning Alliance Synthesis Report," Final Report: *A Multidimensional Analysis of Local and Regional Procurement of US Food Aid*, Cornell University Working Paper, January 2012.

by the Cargo Preference Act, P.L. 83-644 (August 26, 1954). This act contains permanent legislation requiring that 50% of the volume of U.S. agricultural commodities financed under U.S. food aid programs must be shipped on U.S.-flag vessels. An amendment to the act in 1985 increased the share that must be shipped on U.S.-flag vessels to 75%; however, the share was again reduced to 50% by another adopted amendment in 2012.

According to the Maritime Administration (MARAD) of the Department of Transportation, Cargo preference laws are intended:[44]

> to provide a revenue base that will retain and encourage a privately owned and operated U.S.-flag merchant marine because the U.S.-flag merchant marine is a vital resource providing: essential sealift capability in wartime or other national emergencies; a cadre of skilled seafarers available in time of national emergencies; and to protect U.S. ocean commerce from total foreign domination and control.

The Commodity Credit Corporation pays the additional freight charges associated with the 50% cargo preference requirement. Excess costs are incurred because freight rates on U.S.-flag vessels are generally higher than on foreign commercial ships.

During the period when a 75% cargo preference share was in effect (1985-2012), MARAD reimbursed the CCC for the "excess" ocean freight costs incurred by complying with the additional 25% requirement. However, MARAD's reimbursement calculation did not include the additional costs incurred for using a vessel over 25 years of age, nor did its reimbursement include bids for which there were no competing foreign-flag bids (a not uncommon occurrence).[45]

Maritime interests generally support cargo preference, but critics argue that it increases the costs of shipping U.S. commodities to poor countries, thus potentially reducing the volume of food aid provided under a fixed funding appropriation. Studies have found that shipments of food aid on U.S.-flag vessels did little to meet the law's objective of helping to maintain a U.S. merchant marine, while adversely affecting operations of the food aid programs, chiefly by raising the cost of ocean transportation and reducing the volume of commodities that can be shipped.[46]

In 2012, when the cargo preference share was permanently reduced from 75% to 50% in the surface transportation reauthorization act, the reduction was enacted as a cost-saving measure.[47] A CBO score of the provision found that the repeal would result in deficit reductions (i.e., savings) of $108 million annually or $540 million over the period 2012-2017.[48] The actual savings, as well as the eventual volume and value, of U.S. food aid is sensitive to fluctuating commodity prices and commercial ocean freight rates.

---

[44] U.S. DOT, MARAD, "Cargo Preference," viewed on May 21, 2014, at http://www.marad.dot.gov/ ships_shipping_landing_page/cargo_preference/Cargo_Preference_Landing_Page.htm.

[45] Elizabeth R. Bageant, Christopher B. Barrett, and Erin Lentz, "Food Aid and Agricultural Cargo Preference," Policy Brief, Cornell University, Charles H. Dyson School of Applied Economics and Management, November 2010.

[46] Elizabeth R. Bageant et al., "Food Aid and Agricultural Cargo Preference," Policy Brief, Cornell University, C.H. Dyson School of Applied Economics and Management, November 2010; and GAO, Cargo Preference Requirements: Objectives Not Met When Applied to Food Aid Programs, September 29, 1994, available at http://archive.gao.gov/ t2pbat2/152624.pdf.

[47] The Moving Ahead for Progress in the 21st Century Act (MAP-21, H.R. 4348, P.L. 112-141).

[48] Congressional Budget Office, Cost estimate for MAP-21, H.R. 4348, June 29, 2012. The cost savings result from a reduction in the reimbursement MARAD makes to the CCC for costs due to higher freight rates on U.S.-flag vessels.

In 2013, Section 602 of the Bipartisan Budget Act of 2013 (P.L. 113-67) repealed the requirement that MARAD reimburse USDA for ocean freight differential associated with the transportation of food aid shipments on U.S.-flag vessels. Again enacted as a cost-saving measure, the repeal, according to CBO estimates, would result in deficit reductions of about $75 million annually or $356 million over the period 2014-2018.[49]

In 2014, a provision was included in the House's Coast Guard and Maritime Transportation Act of 2014 (H.R. 4005, Section 318) to repeal the reduction in the cargo preference requirement in P.L. 112-41 and to reinstate the provision requiring that 75% of U.S. food aid be shipped on U.S.-flag vessels. The Senate has yet to take any action on this bill.

The Administration's Food Aid Reform Proposal[50]

In advance of the 2014 farm bill, the Administration proposed dramatic changes to the structure and intent of U.S. international food assistance, especially involving Food for Peace Title II resources, including shifting funds from Food for Peace to three USAID accounts authorized in foreign assistance legislation, eliminating the monetization procedure, providing greater flexibility to procure commodities in local and regional markets overseas, and reducing the volume of commodities subject to cargo preference legislation.

Several of these reform proposals were included as part of the Administration's FY2014 budget request. While the 2014 farm bill made some modest changes to international food aid programs, it did not adopt the larger Administration reform proposals. However, USDA and USAID continue to advocate for the Administration's reform agenda. In its FY2015 budget request, the Administration again proposes reforms to U.S. international food assistance programs. Both the FY2014 and FY2015 reform proposals, along with opponents' criticisms, are described below.

Reforms Proposed in the FY2014 Budget Request

In its FY2014 budget request, the Administration proposed to replace funding previously requested for Food for Peace (P.L. 480) Title II, estimated at $1.47 billion annually, with an equivalent amount divided among three USAID assistance accounts as follows:

- ***Shift $1.1 billion to International Disaster Assistance (IDA) for emergency food response***. This shift would have augmented IDA's Emergency Food Security Program, previously described, which provides up to $300 million for cash-based food security assistance (e.g., local and regional procurement, vouchers, or cash transfers). The total available for IDA emergency food security assistance after such a shift would be $1.4 billion.

- ***Shift $250 million to Development Assistance (DA) for a Community Development and Resilience Fund (CDRF)***. The CDRF would address chronic food insecurity in areas of recurrent crises such as in the Horn of Africa or the West African Sahel. The CDRF also would receive $80 million of DA from

---

[49] CBO, Cost Estimate, Bipartisan Budget Act of 2013, as posted on the website of the House Committee on Rules on December 20, 2013.

[50] See USAID's Food Aid Reform website for more discussion of the proposal at http://www.usaid.gov/foodaidreform.

USAID's Bureau of Food Security, which administers the Feed the Future program. Total funding for this program after such a shift would be $330 million.

- ***Shift $75 million to a new Emergency Food Assistance Contingency Fund (EFAC).*** EFAC would serve as a fund to provide emergency food assistance for unexpected and urgent food needs.

USAID argued that the proposed shifts would result in gains of flexibility, timeliness, and efficiency in the provision of emergency food aid that would allow U.S. international food assistance to reach at least 2 to 4 million more people each year with equivalent funding. Rather than a commodity-only response, USAID would be able to select from a menu of options that could include local or regional procurement in countries or regions where food aid emergencies are occurring, and other forms of cash-based assistance like food vouchers or cash transfers.

The CDRF would continue to engage U.S. private voluntary organizations (PVOs) as implementing partners of nonemergency development programs. In addition, USAID argued that the $330 million in the CDRF would be the equivalent of the safe box guarantee because of cost savings associated with the end of monetization.

According to USAID, the food aid reform proposal would guarantee that in FY2014 no less than 55% of the requested $1.4 billion for emergency food assistance would be used for procurement, transport, and related costs of U.S. commodities. Going forward, USAID said that U.S. commodities would continue to make up a significant portion of purchases, especially for many processed foods and bulk commodity procurements, which might not be available elsewhere in the world. Further, inflation concerns or food price volatility may make U.S. commodities a more feasible option.

USAID cited GAO's estimate that monetization loses an average of 25 cents for each dollar of food aid monetized. As a result, USAID argued that by ending monetization, U.S. development food assistance could reach an estimated 800,000 more malnourished people. In addition, "efficiency savings" obtained from the transfer of Food for Peace funds would be devoted to an increase of $25 million to the Maritime Security Program (MSP), administered by MARAD, thus serving as a partial offset for reduced shipping related to smaller U.S. food aid shipments. Efficiency savings would come from shipping fewer commodities overseas. Increasing the direct subsidies to the maritime sector with additional MSP funding was intended to help retain militarily useful U.S.-flag vessels and facilitate the retention of mariners in the workforce.

Criticisms of the FY2014 Reform Proposal

Critics of the Administration's food aid reform proposal included the Alliance for Global Food Security, an organization representing 13 PVOs that have been involved in implementing Food for Peace nonemergency programs and one group that advocates for U.S. food aid policies. The U.S. maritime sector also was critical of the Administration's FY2014 food aid proposal.

In early 2013, prior to the release of the Administration's FY2014 proposal, a group of 70 organizations who supported the current food aid program wrote the President a letter urging continuation of the Food for Peace and other U.S. food aid programs.[51] Then, in response to the

---

[51] Letter to the President from 70 NGO and industry associations in support of current food aid programs, February 21, 2013, viewed at http://www.acdivoca.org/site/Lookup/Support-for-US-Food-Aid-Letter-to-the-President/$file/Support- (continued...)

Administration proposal, the Alliance for Global Food Security recommended the continuation of the current food aid procurement system, rather than diverting Food for Peace appropriations for non-U.S. commodity procurement.[52]

Successful elements of the U.S. procurement system, according to the Alliance, include early warnings, competitive bidding for commodities, monitoring of orders and deliveries, and pre-positioning overseas of U.S. commodities. The Alliance also included the use of IDA funds for local/regional procurement or cash-based assistance pending arrival of either pre-positioned Food for Peace commodities or deliveries of commodities from the United States as a successful component of the U.S. food aid procurement system. The Alliance supports increased funding "as needed" for IDA-funded cash-based food security assistance.

Based on case studies in five countries with monetization programs, the Alliance maintains that the practice provides benefits other than the cash generated to finance PVO projects.[53] Those include increased economic activity that helps alleviate credit, hard currency, or small-volume constraints that limit procurement of sufficient food supplies on international markets. An Alliance recommendation related to monetization was that USAID's Development Assistance (DA) funds be used to support Food for Peace Title II development programs where monetization is not "feasible or appropriate."

USA Maritime—an organization that represents shipper and maritime unions—also opposed transforming the current food aid programs from a commodity-based to a cash-based program. It argued that the Administration's proposed food aid changes would put at risk a food aid program that has the support of farmers, international relief and development organizations, ports, and inland and ocean transporters.[54] USA Maritime also argued that the cargo preference mandated for U.S. food aid exports contributes to the maintenance and retention of a strong merchant marine, and that the combination of handling, processing, and transporting U.S. international food aid from the farm to foreign ports supports substantial economic activity.[55]

Catholic Relief Services is not a member of the Alliance for Global Food Security, and has been supportive of the Administration's proposal.[56] However, its support is contingent on there being a long-term authorization of the reforms, not an annual appropriation. Catholic Relief Services' public donor group director indicated in a press briefing that "the set of reforms offers a great deal of flexibility and ways to make food aid programming more efficient and to enable us to use our local purchase mechanism to support the local farmer and household which needs food ... [b]ut the concern we are raising is that there's got to be an authorizing framework in place to make sure that it's a consistent program available year upon year."

(...continued)

for-US-Food-Aid-Letter-to-the-President.pdf.

[52] Alliance for Global Food Security, "Briefing Paper: Recommended Components of a Food Aid Reform Package," April 10, 2013, viewed at http://foodaid.org/news/wp-content/uploads/2013/04/AGFS-Food-Aid-Reform-Recommendations-4-10-13.pdf.

[53] Informa Economics, *op.cit.*

[54] USA Maritime, "Statement of USA Maritime on Proposed Changes to the Food for Peace Program (PL-480)", April 24, 2013, viewed at http://bridgedeck.org/forms/USA-Maritime-Food-for-Peace-press-release-24-April-2013.pdf.

[55] Promar International, *Impacts on the U.S. Economy of Shipping International Food Aid*, a report prepared for USA Maritime, June 2010, viewed at http://mebaunion.org/WHATS-NEW/Food_Aid-April_2010.pdf.

[56] "Catholic agency hopes for lasting food aid reform," posted by CNA Daily News on April 21, 2013, viewed at http://www.dfwcatholic.org/catholic-agency-hopes-for-lasting-food-aid-reform-51941/ html.

Jurisdictional Issues Associated with Reform Proposals

USAID's FY2014 food aid reform proposal raised issues of congressional committee and subcommittee jurisdiction over food aid appropriations and authorizing legislation. In the Senate, food aid authorizing legislation has been with the Agriculture, Nutrition and Forestry Committee, while appropriations jurisdiction has been with the Agriculture Appropriations Subcommittee. In the House, jurisdiction over authorizing legislation has been with the Agriculture Committee, periodically shared with the Foreign Affairs Committee. Appropriations have been in the purview of the Agriculture Appropriations Subcommittee. Shifting food aid funding to programs authorized in foreign assistance legislation (e.g., IDA and DA) as proposed by the Administration suggests that responsibility for food aid appropriations would be shifted to Foreign Operations Appropriations Subcommittees in both chambers and that, going forward, authorizing legislation would become the responsibility of House Foreign Affairs and Senate Foreign Relations Committees.

Reforms Proposed in the FY2015 Budget Request

Although the 2014 farm bill made some modest changes to U.S. international food assistance, it failed to adopt the Administration's more dramatic reform proposals. In a revised version of its international food aid reform efforts, the President's FY2015 budget proposal seeks additional flexibility for Title II emergency programs by requesting that up to 25% of Title II resources be available for interventions such as local and regional procurement of commodities, food vouchers, or cash transfers.[57] USAID claims that the cost savings and improved timeliness associated with a shift in use of Title II funds from shipping U.S. commodities on U.S.-flag vessels to cash transfers or local and regional purchases would allow USAID to reach an additional 2 million people.[58]

As under its FY2014 budget request, the Administration again proposes that a portion of the "efficiency savings" obtained from the transfer of Food for Peace funds would be devoted to an annual increase of $25 million to the Maritime Security Program (MSP), administered by MARAD, thus serving as a partial offset for reduced shipping related to smaller U.S. food aid shipments.

---

[57] USAID fact sheet, "The Future of Food Assistance: U.S. Food Aid Reform," available at http://www.usaid.gov/news-information/fact-sheets/future-food-assistance-us-food-aid-reform-fy2015.

[58] USAID fact sheet, "Food Aid Reform: Behind the Numbers," available at http://www.usaid.gov/sites/default/files/documents/1869/FoodAidReform_BehindtheNumbers.pdf.

Author Contact Information

Randy Schnepf
Specialist in Agricultural Policy
rschnepf@crs.loc.gov, 7-4277

Acknowledgments

Charles Hanrahan, retired, and Melissa D. Ho, formerly with CRS, co-authored an earlier version of this report.